I Tickled My Teachers

58 Hilariously Heartful School Poems

poems by Ted Scheu
photographs by Peter Lourie

Young
Poets'
Press

MIDDLEBURY, VT

I Tickled My Teachers
Second Edition, December 2009

Text copyright © 2007 by Ted Scheu
Photographs copyright © 2007 by Peter Lourie
Design by Winslow Colwell/WColwell Design

Published in the United States by Young Poets' Press
PO Box 564, Middlebury, VT 05753
www.youngpoetspress.com

Grateful acknowledgement is made to the publishers of the following publications in which work previously appeared:

"Lost and Found" originally appeared in the anthology *Rolling in the Aisles*, 2004, Meadowbrook Press.

"Cursive Curse," "F's are Fabulous," and "Testing, testing, testing!" originally appeared in the anthology *If Kids Ruled the School*, 2004, Meadowbrook Press.

"Chicken Parts," and "The Rules For This Assembly" originally appeared in the anthology *My Teacher's in Detention*, 2006, Meadowbrook Press.

The text of this publication was set in American Typewriter.

ISBN 978-0-9825499-2-6
Library of Congress Control Number: 2007937696

This book is dedicated
to all hard-working,
laugh-launching, school kids
(and the teachers who inspire them)

With special thanks to the kids and administrators
at the C.P. Smith and H.O. Wheeler Schools
in Burlington, Vermont who helped
with the project.

Table of Contents

I Love Mondays 1
Today 2
Nancy Cristman Kissed Me. 4
Testing, testing, testing! 7
How Can I Be Quiet? 9
First Day, New School 10
I Tickled My Teachers 12
A Little Smelly 14
With My Compliments 17
The Most Embarrassing 3-Letter Word 18
I Refuse to Smile 19
Worst of Friends 20
Yo, Columbus! 22
Cursive Curse. 25
the poem with the longest title 26
Backwards Walking Day 28
Day Talking Backwards. 29
The Rules for this Assembly. 31
Pull-ups Are Awesome 32
A Better Report Card 35
I'm Planning a Serious Stomach Ache 36
I'll Eat Just Half. 37
Dear Teacher, ... 39
Teacher Appreciation Week 40
I Promise. 43
My Place to Fly 44
Apo'strophe's 46
Time Can Fly 47
Talking Tough 49
"F" is for "Fabulous" 50

Special Thanks to George and Abe 52

Interrupting 54

Memory Aid 56

Nose Tip. 57

The Four Food Groups 59

Classroom Fashion King 60

"Do Over!" 62

I'm the Fastest 65

My New...Um...Invention 66

A Most Amazing Miracle 67

Arithmetic Friends 68

My High Tech Teacher 71

Parent-Teacher Conference 72

Rotten Eggs 75

Chicken Parts 77

Hide and Seek 79

My Fast Fantastic Field Trip 80

I've Brought a Guest to School Today 82

Science Un-Fair 85

The Duke of Dodgeball 87

Reciting a Poem in Front
    of My Whole School 88

Lost and Found 91

Ooops 92

Someday 93

Overdue 95

The Weekend is Coming 96

Aaaaa! 99

Summer Brains 100

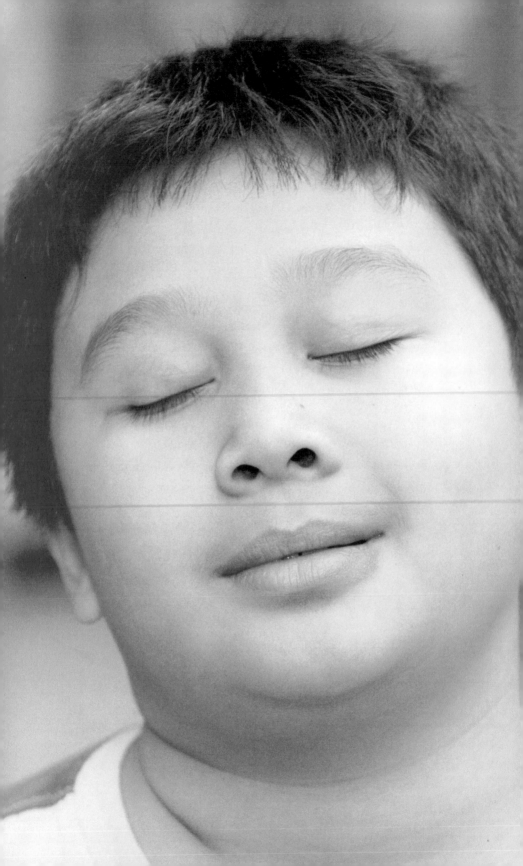

I Love Mondays

The weekend's finally over,
and you might think it's cruel
that I and lots of other kids
are heading back to school.

But I can't wait to get there—
it's time that I confessed
that school's the only place I've found
where I can get some rest.

Today

Today I am the sharpest kid
the world has ever known.
I'm wicked hot and super cool—
completely "in the zone."

Today I know that I could leap
the tallest mountain peak.
And I could swim around the world
in just about a week.

Today I'm feeling faster than
a cheetah chasing dinner.
And if I ran for president
I know I'd be the winner.

Today my brain is brighter than
a beam of laser light.
My heart is soaring higher than
a wild flying kite.

Today I even might recite
a billion books by heart.
And all because my teacher stopped
and told me I was smart.

Nancy Cristman Kissed Me

Nancy Cristman kissed me
as we walked to school today.
It happened fast and I was lost
with what to do or say.

I quickly looked around to check
if anyone had seen it.
If they did, and tease me,
they'll be sorry, and I mean it.

Why did Nancy Cristman put
that smack upon my cheek?
I'm so confused and probably
will stay this way all week.

I'll guess I'll have to marry her
and share my lemonade.
A lot can happen to a kid
who walks to second grade.

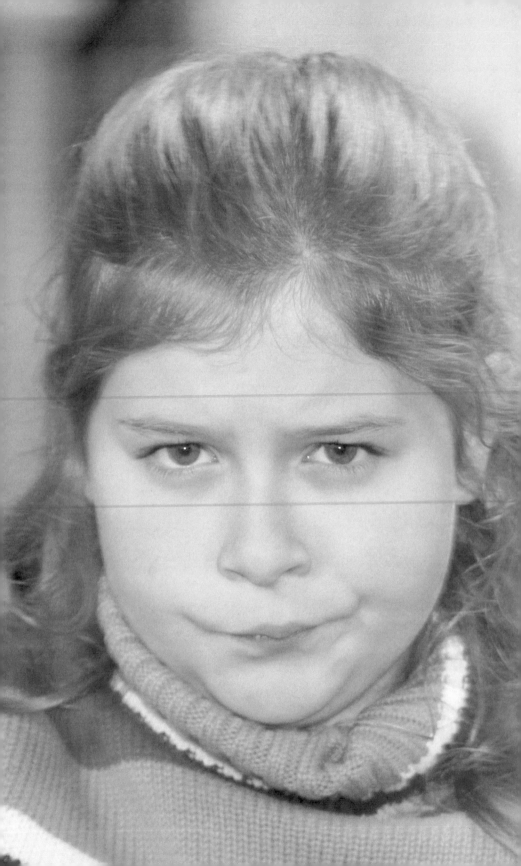

Testing, testing, testing!

Testing, testing, testing!
They're testing us to death.
At school we take so many tests
we're almost out of breath,

From testing, testing, testing!
It's all we seem to do.
If you could look inside our brains
you'd see they're black and blue,

From testing, testing, testing!
And that is my concern—
We take so many tests each week
there's never time to learn.

How Can I Be Quiet?

They're taking tests upstairs today
so, downstairs, we must walk
as silently as sleepy slugs
and whisper when we talk.

But I can hardly hide inside
my happiness and glee.
I want to scream and share my joy
that they aren't testing me.

First Day, New School

Soon, I'm sure, I'll make some friends
and even learn their names.
And soon I'll be included,
out at recess, in some games.

Soon I'll learn the schedule—
like when we stop for snack,
and when we shuffle off to gym,
and when they drag us back.

I'll learn the short-cuts in the halls
for walking more directly.
And hopefully my teacher will
pronounce my name correctly.

I'll even, someday, show my class
that I'm a science whiz.
But, most of all, extremely soon
(before I pop like a balloon)
I'll find out where the bathroom is.

I Tickled My Teachers

I tickled each of my teachers today;
you should have seen their eyes.
I never thought a teacher's face
could show so much surprise.

Tickling teachers is usually
a dangerous thing to do.
But when you hear how well it worked
you'll want to try it too.

It doesn't take a special skill
but, prob'ly, you should know
I never used my finger and
I never touched a toe.

Instead, I said, "good morning" as
I slid into my seat.
And when we wrote, I strained to make
my letters extra neat.

I raised my hand politely and
I didn't stomp or yell.
I kept my snake inside its box
at morning show and tell.

I took my turn at recess and
I never slid in mud.
I didn't spill the ketchup and
pretend that it was blood.

I didn't push a single kid
or cut a single line.
And when I didn't get my way
I almost didn't whine.

This sounds a little crazy but
it's absolutely true.
My teachers all were smiling by
the time the day was through.

But tickling teachers is tiring too,
and harder than I thought.
So, will I tickle tomorrow again?
Absolutely! (Not!)

A Little Smelly

A little smelly caught my nose
in class the other day.
It lingered long around my desk
and wouldn't go away.

I quickly asked my neighbors
"who made that little stink?"
But they just shrugged their eyebrows
and blinked a little wink.

That little smelly hung around—
just floating near my chair.
"Don't look at **me**! Stop laughing!
It wasn't me, I swear!"

I learned a stinky lesson when
it finally cleared away:
if you smell a little smelly
for heaven's sake don't say.

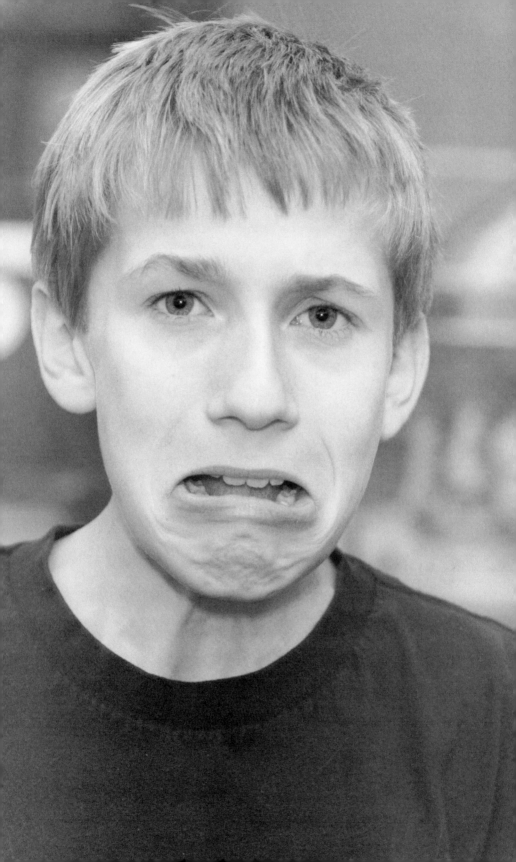

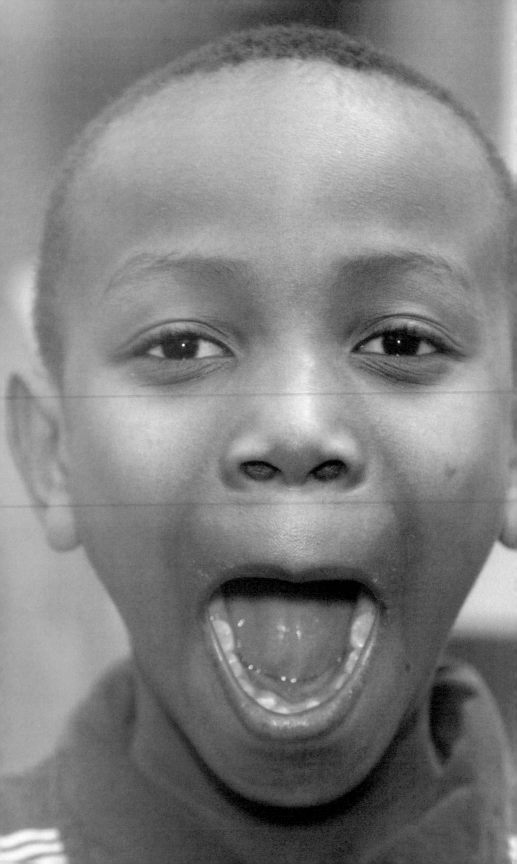

With My Compliments

"Great idea! You're the smartest!
You're the kid who works the hardest!
Fine decision! Perfect choice!
I love the wisdom in your voice!
Super haircut! Awesome clothes!
Your taste and coolness clearly shows!
I'll pat your back! And shake your hand!
Hire you a marching band!
Yes, you're the best in all you do!
I hope, someday, to be like you!"

I am the King of Compliments,
as you can clearly see.
And every single compliment
is meant for only **me**!

The Most Embarrassing 3-Letter Word to Ever Utter in a Quiet Classroom

My brain is wobbling wildly.
My face is blooming red.
I'd pay a billion dollars to
unsay what I just said.

The teasing is increasing as
I struggle to stay calm.
I don't know why my tongue and I
just called my teacher "Mom."

I Refuse to Smile

No matter how hard
this school photographer
tries to get me to laugh
I refuse to do it.

I'll say the words
he tells me like
"Cheese Whiz!"
"Pepperoni Pizza!"
"Boogerberry Breath!"
"There's Dog Doo on My Shoe!"
and
"Oh no! My epidermis is showing!"
But I won't crack
a smile for him.
No way.

I see he's getting angry now.
He's looking at the long line of kids
and then back at me.
Then he tells me to say the words
"This is the absolute stupidest,
most boring thing I'll ever do!"

I say it and nod my head
and smile, because it's true.
That's when he snaps my picture.
What a dirty trick.

Worst of Friends

Joe and I are worst of friends—
we like it best that way.
We see each other coming
and walk the other way.

I give him grief about his clothes
and he just laughs at mine.
We drive each other crazy
and agree that that's just fine.

He tells me I am "stupid."
I smile and say "You're dumb!"
It warms us both to see
what ugly friends we have become.

I'm always there to scowl at him
and he is there for me.
It's kind of nice to know for now
that's how it's going to be.

And, maybe, in a week or two
we'll tire of being petty.
Then we'll become best friends again—
but, right now?

We're not ready.

Yo, Columbus!

Columbus sailed
the ocean blue.
His trip became
a dream come true.

Because he made it
all that way,
they keep us out
of school today.

So, Columbus,
I'm your biggest fan.
Yo, Christopher baby,
you're the man.

Cursive Curse

My "m's" are much too bumpy.
My "u's" are far too lumpy.
My "k's" are way too droopy.
My "l's" are all too loopy.
My "e's" are "i's," and "i's" are "e's."
My "z's" have got some rare disease.
My tails are tilted to the right.
My "x" is not a handsome sight.
My wimpy "r's" are worst of all;
the bumps on top are much too small.

My pencil shouts to stop for air.
My hand is sore, this isn't fair.
My teacher doesn't understand—
I'll *never* have a steady hand.
I feel a need to scream, or worse.
So, close your ears, or you may hear
a bumpy-lumpy,
droopy-loopy,
wimpy-skimpy,
cursive curse.

this is the poem with the longest
title in the universe all because
we have to write a 150 word
poem tonight for homework and
our teacher made the really big
mistake of telling us that the rules
for writing poems are different
than for regular writing so that we
are completely in charge of how
our poems look and we can even
leave off punctuation and capital
letters if we want to and we can
even make super long titles i hope
and make it rhyme if we want to
even though she very strongly
suggested against rhyming because
it is less beautiful and besides i
really really really really hate
writing poems i don't know why
exactly because they are actually
very easy to write so this is what
i have decided to do in order to
complete the assignment here is
my poem

no fun
im done

Backwards Walking Day

Today is Backwards Walking Day
if anybody cares.
You have to backwards-walk the halls
and up and down the stairs.

Every step is in reverse
no matter where you go.
Until you get the hang of it
you'll have to take it slow.

You mustn't ever turn around—
I'm sorry, that's the rule.
It took an hour and seven falls
for me to walk to school.

But it was worth it just to feel
that sense of celebration
that soon will race, at breakneck pace,
clear across our nation.

It sounds a little weird I know
but there is nothing to it.
And think of all the laughs we'll have
watching teachers do it.

So here's to you, and everyone,
who tries to walk this way.
And don't forget tomorrow
is Backwards Talking Day!

Day Talking Backwards

—day talking backwards is Today
.down upside turned day a
half a and week a for laugh will mouth Your
.around flipped are words when

,and ,sandwich a of outside jelly Like
,bun its surrounding dog hot a
day whole one backwards talking
.fun and sticky and tricky is

boost a brain and tongue your give So
.lazy too get won't they so
and giggles of grunch a get You'll
!crazy go may teacher your

The Rules for this Assembly
(As explained by our very silly principal)

"Raise your hand
if you're not here.
Do it now,
sometime next year.

"Please don't move,
except to wiggle.
Do not laugh,
except to giggle.

"Sit up tall
so you can't see.
Buy a ticket,
they are free.

"Close your mouth
and say "hello."
Quickly do it,
very slow.

"Let's all cry
and have some fun.
We'll start as soon
as we are done."

Pull-ups Are Awesome

We had to do pull-ups
this morning in Gym.
I knew, as I got there
my chances were slim.

My mouth was a desert.
My fingers were sweaty.
My legs were like rubbery
soggy spaghetti.

With everyone gaping
I leapt for the bar.
I tugged and I struggled
but didn't get far.

And just when I thought
I would drop in a pile,
I turned and saw Sally Smith
giggle and smile.

I stopped when I'd counted
to seventy-four.
And I'm pretty certain
I could've done more.

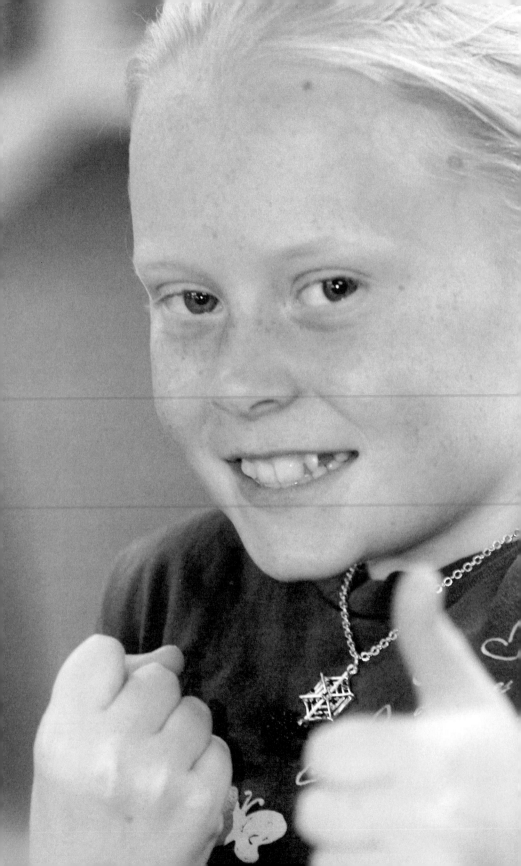

A Better Report Card

I dragged my new report card home;
it seemed to weigh a ton.
"Next time," my parents growled at me,
"bring back a better one."

So when our grades arrived next time
I really used my head.
I borrowed a card from my smartest friend
and brought hers home instead.

I'm Planning a Serious Stomach Ache

I'm planning
a serious stomach ache.
A short one
would be best.

I'll have it
after recess
and before
my spelling test.

I'll Eat Just Half

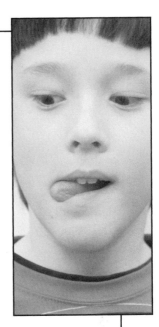

I brought a candy bar for snack
but I can't eat it all.
Although my eyes are pretty wide
my stomach's feeling small.

I know it sounds surprising,
and nearly makes me laugh,
but since I'm not that hungry now
I'm going to eat just half.

I'll hide the rest inside my desk
and totally ignore
those dark, delicious flavors that
I savor and adore.

It's almost irresistible—
so fudgy and delightful.
My tortured tongue is crying out
to taste a tiny biteful.

But I will save this other half;
that is my solemn vow.
I'll eat it sometime later...

I think it's later now.

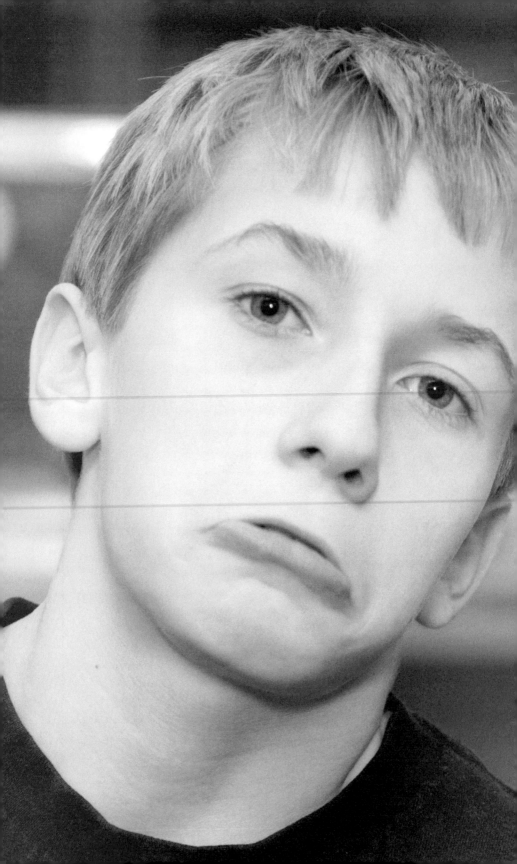

Dear Teacher,

I had the *best* excuse today
explaining clearly why
I couldn't do my homework—
a *perfect* alibi.

The note was neatly written in
my mother's careful hand.
I won't reveal the things it said—
I knew you'd understand.

It was the best excuse *by far*—
I won't exaggerate it.
I'd love to show it to you, but
my stupid puppy ate it.

Teacher Appreciation Week

It's Teacher Appreciation Week—
a time to launch a cheer
for all the fun, amazing stuff
we've learned with them this year.

We've showered them with chocolates,
and flowers by the bunches,
and all our moms are thanking them
with extra-yummy lunches.

Our hands are stained with marker ink
from making cards and signs.
For once, on mine, I even kept
my words between the lines.

I guess our teachers do deserve
this week of thanks and fuss.
Now, I can't wait to celebrate
the week when they thank **us**.

I Promise

Cross my kidneys,
hope to cry.
Stick a pickle
in my eye.

Cross my guts
from head to toes.
Poke bananas
up my nose.

Cross my liver,
cross my hips.
Secrets never
cross my lips.

Cross my body,
every part.
Your secret's safe,
I cross my heart.

I will never tell a soul
until my body's stiff and cold.
Except the kids at recess
who I already told.

My Place to Fly

The library
is where I go
to launch myself and fly.

I swoop and loop
above the earth
a thousand stories high.

Apo'strophe's

I never quite remember where
apo'strophe's 'should go.
My teacher alway's roll's her eye's
and tell's me, "You 'should know!"

When I am 'sure I under'stand,
I alway's do it wrong.
And looking up the rule in book's
ju'st take's me way too long.

It's all about po's'se's'sion,
but that i's too confu'sing.
'So I de'signed a 'special trick
you 'see that Ive been u'sing.

I never need to take a chance,
and never have to gue's's.
I drop in one apo'strophe
in front of every 's!

Time Can Fly

We turned our clocks ahead last night—
my parents made the changes.
Of all the silly things they do
it maybe is the strangest.

I'll never fully understand
the reason that we do it.
An hour of my life was gone
before I even knew it.

If they can change the time of day,
then I can do it too.
I quietly decided
what I was going to do.

I waited till I got to school
and halfway through my morning,
when, quicker than a hummingbird,
without a word of warning,

I scampered to the classroom clock
when teacher turned her back.
And suddenly, we kids announced
that it was time for snack.

It worked so well, I waited for
our spelling test to start.
I turned the clock ahead again
and it was time for art.

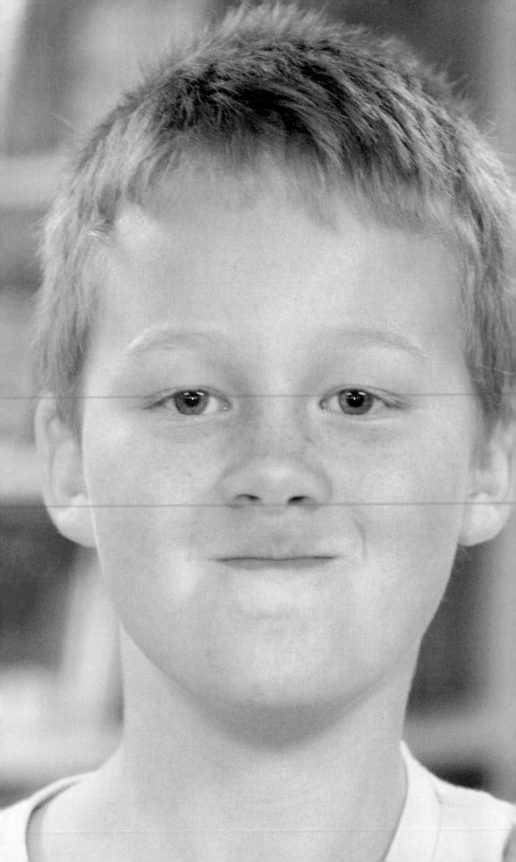

Talking Tough

"Listen, Buddy!
That's right. I'm talkin' to you!
You may think you're tough,
but you're nothin' but a cream puff.
You picked a fight with the wrong kid today, buster.
You may look big mean and difficult,
but I can beat you with one hand behind my back.
By my calculations, you're history, bubba.
You may be a problem for most kids,
but you don't scare me one bit.
I've got your number, my friend.
I'm gonna divide you into pieces
and when I'm through with you
you'll just be an answer to my prayers.
You understand?
Go ahead.
Show me what you've got.
I'm ready."

Sometimes you just have to talk tough
to a math problem.

"F" is for "Fabulous"

Hey, Mom and Dad! I got my grades!
And you'll be thrilled to hear
the marks on our report cards
are changed around this year.

A bunch of kids were telling me
this morning on the bus
that they had heard some teachers say
that "F's" are "Fabulous."

And "D's" are proudly given out
for work that's "Dynamite."
They're used to honor kids like me
whose brains are wicked bright.

A "C" of course is super "Cool"—
I've got a few of those.
I wish they could be "D's" and "F's"
but that's the way it goes.

I'm pleased to see my teacher
didn't give an "A" or "B."
I've worked too hard for one of those—
Gosh, aren't you proud of me?

I see you don't believe me.
You think that I am lying?
At least you will agree
that I should get an "A" for trying!

Special Thanks to George and Abe

To Washington and Lincoln—
two leaders of our nation,
I offer up this poem
in humble dedication.

When their birthdays come around
I'll lead the celebration
to send these two amazing men
my thanks and admiration.

Let's give Old George and Honest Abe
a thundering ovation,
for my favorite February days...
vacation.

Interrupting

Interrupting makes me mad.
It's totally unfair.
Like someone stole your place in line
when you were standing there.

Interrupting's impolite—
a thoughtless thing to do.
So kindly lock your little lips
and wait till I am through.

Interrupting's rude and crass—
the lowest of the low.
And while I'm on the subject,
there's more you need to know.

Interrupting's ugly
and totally dismaying.
Oh, I'm sorry...
what were you saying?

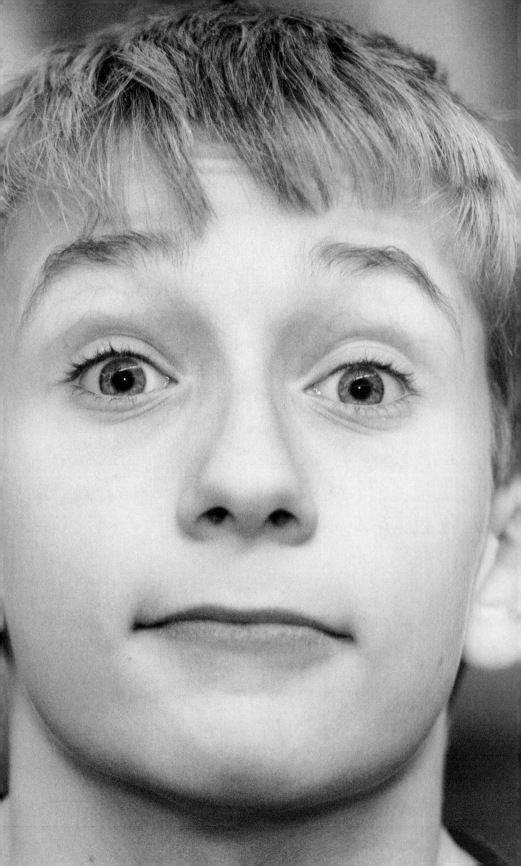

Memory Aid

My memory is horrible—
I never have a clue.
I can't remember when, or where,
or what, or why, or who?

My teacher had a great idea—
a notebook where I write
the stuff I need to focus on
for homework every night.

So now I will be ready
for every test and quiz,
if only I'd remember where
my silly notebook is.

Nose Tip

Here's a quick
and nifty tip
and I suggest
you follow it.

Don't giggle when
you drink your milk
unless, at first,
you swallow it.

The Four Food Groups

We saw a pyramid in school
about the foods that we should eat.
The best of all, our teacher said,
are veggies, grains, and things like meat.

Sugar was the final food—
the kind to eat the least of.
But that's the stuff, when I get home,
I always make a feast of.

I thought about that pyramid
extremely hard and long.
No matter how I stacked it up
it seemed completely wrong.

I told my teacher I was sure
that she was way off track.
The most important groups for me
are breakfast, dinner, lunch, and snack.

Classroom Fashion King

I never have the coolest clothes
and every day I show it.
The kids with all the cooler clothes
are quick to let me know it.

They laugh because my pants are short
and tease my choice of shirt.
I try to just ignore their jeers
but, honestly, they hurt.

And then, last night, some movie star
appeared on our TV.
I couldn't quite believe it but
he dressed the same as me.

Today when I arrived in class
I had to rub my eyes.
Before me sat a bunch of kids
I barely recognized.

Their pants were short and every shirt
was weird in its design.
I giggled when I realized
their clothes were just like mine.

They all pretended they were cool
and didn't say a thing.
But it was clear that I was now
the classroom fashion king.

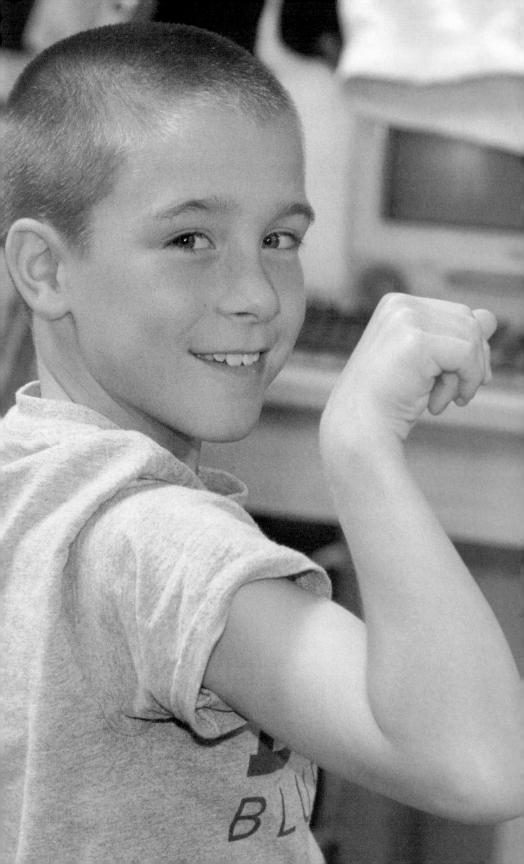

"Do Over!"

Whenever things don't go my way,
I have two words I always say,

"Do Over!"

So then I get a second try.
And if I lose, I simply cry,

"Do Over!"

If I strike out or miss the ball,
I laugh, and very quickly call,

"Do Over!"

It's such a waste of time to pout
when all you have to do is shout,

"Do Over!"

So when I blew my spelling test,
I told my teacher — yep, you guessed,

"Do Over!"

And then I got to sit and write
for nearly half a day and night,
a thousand times and maybe more,
until my hand was sad and sore
I wrote, "It almost never pays,
in school, to use that stupid phrase,

"Do Over!"

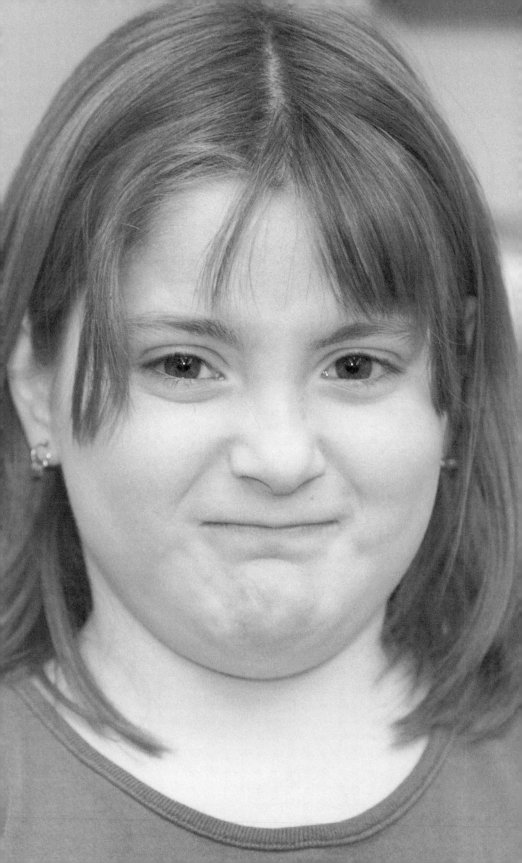

I'm The Fastest

I'm the fastest in my class.
I prove it every day.
No one's quite as quick as me
in one amazing way.

I think it's time to tell you so
you're not the last to know.
It's hard to hold my pride inside.
I need to let it show.

I find it kind of funny but
my teacher's not amused.
I'm always fastest in my class
at being most confused.

My New...Um...Invention

I have a new...um...invention
that I have just...um...designed.
I'd love to share it with you...um...now
if you don't...um...mind.

It keeps the raindrops off the...um...heads
of every...um...gal and...um...fella.
I bet you'd love to get one...um...soon.
I call it my...um...brella.

A Most Amazing Miracle

A most amazing miracle
occurred in school today.
I didn't quite deserve it but
it happened anyway.

We had to read our book report,
but I had not completed it.
I'd hoped to find some extra time
for, heaven knows, I needed it.

I told my class I'd finished mine
so I would not look dumb.
But when my teacher called on me
the time for truth had come.

I felt the heat beneath my feet
like burgers on a grill.
But just as I got up to speak
we had a fire drill!

Pretending I was angry
I said a quiet prayer,
then staggered out into the sun
to grab a gulp of air.

A book report is not a thing
that gets me too excited.
But just in case my luck runs out,
I think tonight I'll write it.

Arithmetic Friends

I'm sorry you are hurting so
and feeling sick and sad.
I wish, inside my head, I'd find
some words that I could add.

I'm feeling awfully awkward.
I'm not sure how to act.
I wish I had a magic wand
to make your pain subtract.

I hurt when you're unhappy.
I cringe to see you cry.
I'd love to find a tiny smile
and make it multiply.

I'll stay until we find one —
on that I am decided.
'Cause we're the kind of friends
that cannot ever be divided.

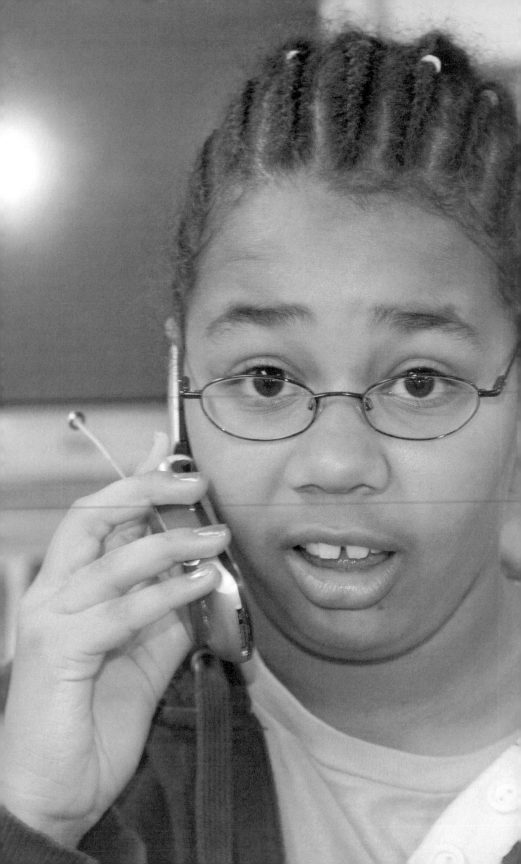

My High Tech Teacher

We've got a high tech classroom—
computerized throughout.
Our teacher sees technologies
as something we can't live without.

Our room is filled with gadgets
that beep and buzz and blink.
I've never met my teacher but
she's pretty nice, I think.

Her face is always on a screen
and that's the way she leads us.
She gave us each a cell phone
and calls us when she needs us.

Parent-Teacher Conference

My homework's always overdue—
it makes my teacher mad.
So she arranged a meeting with
my mother and my dad.

I know she wants to ask them both
why I procrastinate.
But she may never get the chance—
my parents both are late.

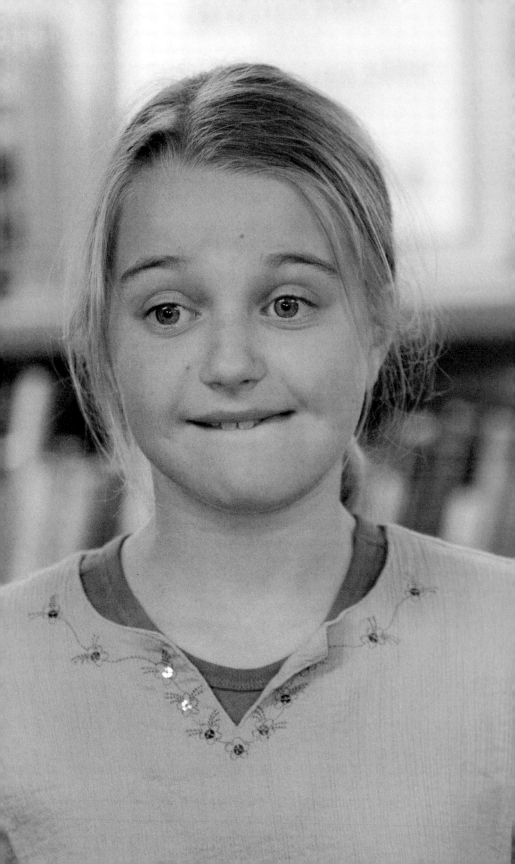

Rotten Eggs

"The last one there's a rotten egg!"
is always fun to say.
I use those words at recess
almost every single day.

But you can get in trouble too,
so let me just remind you:
don't shout those words unless there is
a slower kid behind you.

Chicken Parts

A picture of a chicken
is in my science book.
Since I am very curious
I stopped and took a look.

Some arrows pointed to the parts—
like wings, and legs, and breast.
I saw the beak, and feet, and tail,
but couldn't find the rest.

I learned a lot about that bird
but, still, the question lingers...
Where are all the nuggets,
and the patties, and the fingers?

Hide and Seek

School's a game
of hide and seek—
that's how some guy
designed it.

We hide an answer
in our brains,
and then we try
to find it.

My Fast Fantastic Field Trip

I took a field trip yesterday—
my teacher never knew.
I slipped outside, and down the street,
directly to the zoo.

The gates were closed, but I snuck in,
with a leap, a pull, and a climb.
For just about an hour
I had the funnest time.

I paddled in the penguins' pool
and slithered with some snakes.
Then thoughtful yaks invited me
for morning tea and cakes.

I joked with five hyenas;
we laughed until we cried.
A couple cordial crocodiles
took me for a ride.

I hung with some gorillas;
we swung between the trees.
I lunched with chummy lions.
Got the latest buzz from bees.

They all insisted I return
tomorrow if I could.
And since they'd been so friendly,
I promised them I would.

I thanked them all politely
then hurried up the street.
No one seemed to notice as
I slid into my seat.

School is mostly pretty cool
but surely you'd agree
a tiny trip inside your mind
makes mornings pass more easily.

I've Brought a Guest to School Today

I've brought a guest to school today—
he's standing by my chair.
I know he looks surprising but
I wish you wouldn't stare.

Although his hair's a little long
and he has tiny feet,
he's just about the nicest guy
you'd ever want to meet.

He doesn't speak our language,
but seems to understand.
He's pretty shy and quiet but
he'd love to shake your hand.

He loves to learn and mostly does
exactly what he's told.
It's really quite amazing since
he isn't very old.

He's handsome as a movie star
from his eyebrows to his toes.
It doesn't seem to matter that
he isn't wearing clothes.

Our teacher hasn't seen him yet
but they'll be meeting soon.
I hope she will agree to let
him stay all afternoon.

The problem is, for him to stay,
we'd have to break a rule.
I'm pretty sure that puppy dogs
are not allowed in school.

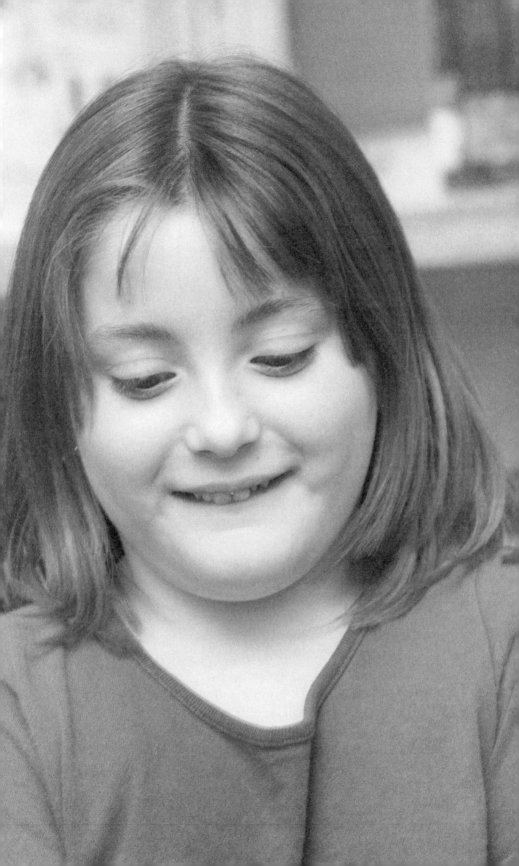

Science Un-Fair

Our Science Fair was held tonight—
I know the guy who won.
The judges were surprised to see
the work that he had done.

I helped him out a teeny bit,
but it was his design.
I liked that he decided to
include me on his sign.

The crowd could not believe it when
we rolled it through the door.
Their eyes were wide in shocked surprise.
their jaws were on the floor.

The thing began to buzz and blink
and smoke began to spew.
It's still a mystery to me
the things that thing could do.

It's true his project was the best
but, still, my friends were mad
when all the teachers turned and gave
the trophy to my dad.

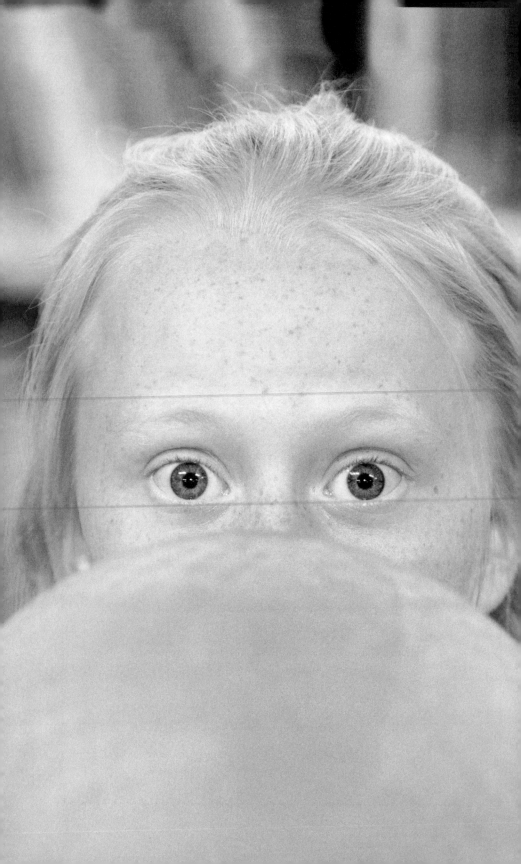

The Duke of Dodgeball

I'm called "The Duke of Dodgeball"—
the greatest in the game.
Against the best, I never rest
at putting bigger kids to shame.

I wear my crown with confidence,
and much to their dismay,
opposing teams have scary dreams
the night before we play.

It's not that I am lightning-quick
or have a rocket throw.
My arms are limp spaghetti and
my feet are turtle-slow.

Instead, I use a strategy
of wiliness and wit.
I hide behind the biggest boys
until they all get hit.

When they go out, I follow them —
I sit and wait, and then,
when all the balls are on our side,
I shout, "Hey, I'm still in!"

So cheer "The Duke of Dodgeball,"
and celebrate my reign.
I'm proud to be, for all to see,
a super royal pain.

Reciting a Poem in Front of My Whole School

(plus a bunch of silly parents too)

I'm standing at this microphone
and see a sea of eyes.
My stomach's doing somersaults
with bouncing butterflies.

I have to say a poem that
I memorized last night.
I hope I sort of, almost,
kind of, nearly get it right.

Although my teacher said
to say it *s l o w* and SCREAMY-LOUD,
my knees are feeling knocky and
my brain is in a cloud.

Maybe in a hundred years
I'll think that this was fun.
But now I'm not so tickled.
And now...HEY WOW!...I'M DONE!

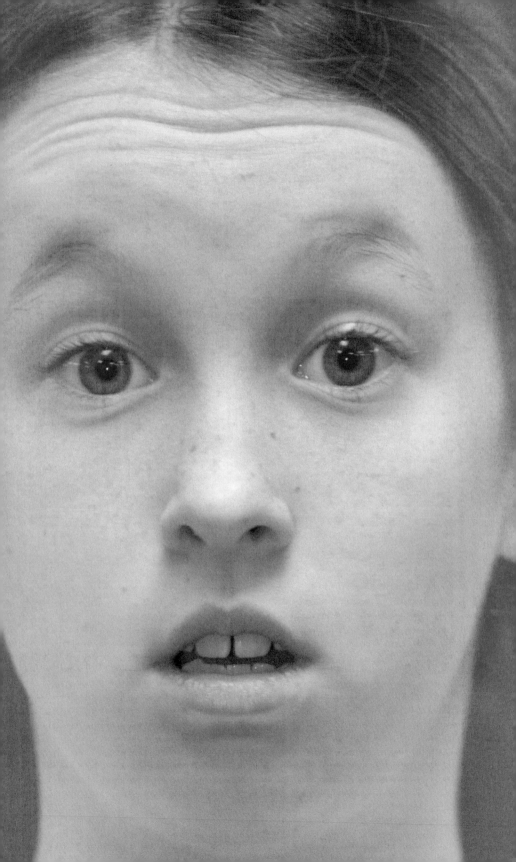

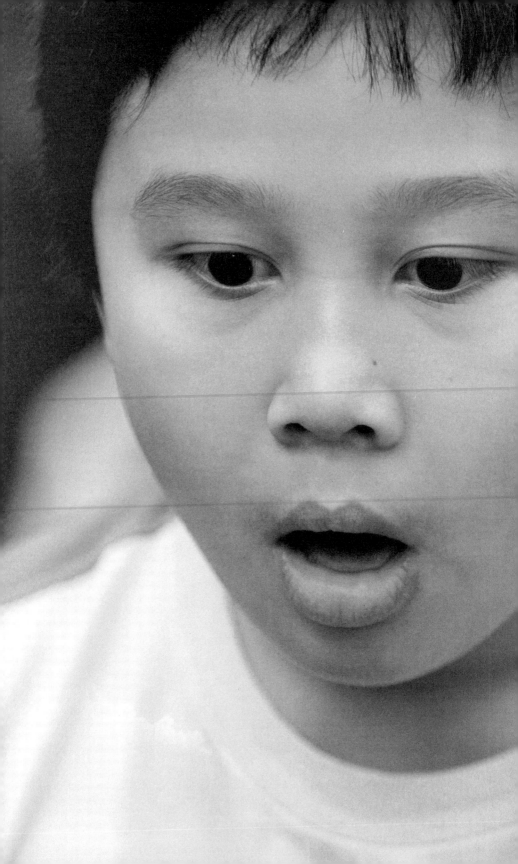

Lost and Found

This morning, Mom reminded me
to check the Lost and Found.
So, just to make her happy,
I took a look around.

The box was like a stinky mouth
whose grin was dark and wide.
I gulped and took a monster breath
then reached my arm inside.

I dug around without a sound
through swirls of clothes and dirt.
To my delight, the box spit out
my favorite soccer shirt.

I peered a little deeper down
and there, to my surprise,
a little face gazed up at me
with wide and eager eyes.

I took a triple-double take
and saw it was my sister.
It's sad to think for several weeks,
we hadn't even missed her.

Ooops

We found a book of magic
and practiced for a year.
We tried to learn a spell to make
our homework disappear.

We waved our special magic wands
and spoke a fancy phrase,
and suddenly our room was filled
with blueish smoke and haze.

When skies had cleared, we sneaked a peek
with wide and wild eyes.
There isn't any class on earth
that felt as much surprise.

Our magic spell had had a sad
and unexpected feature:
Our homework list was twice as long,
and we had lost our teacher.

Someday

Someday I'll be the president
and bring the world together.
Or, as a famous scientist,
I'll help to change the weather.

I'll bet I may compose, someday,
a famous symphony.
Or make a ton of money
and give it all away.

Someday I'll write a poem
that makes a child smile.
And, maybe, I will even be
a teacher for a while.

I'll be a great explorer too,
and climb the highest mountain.
But first, I hope I grow enough
to reach the water fountain.

Overdue

This morning I
was in a stew—
I learned my mouth
was overdue.

Lately, it's
been working great—
I didn't think
to check the date.

So when I tried
and couldn't talk,
I grabbed my voice
and took a walk.

Down the hallway
rapidly,
I led my head
to the library.

The librarian stamped
my tongue and cheeks,
so I can talk
for two more weeks.

The Weekend is Coming

The weekend is coming—
I'm counting it down.
The mouth on my face is
no longer a frown.

The weekend is coming—
I'm feeling it's true.
I noticed my teacher
is smiling too.

The weekend is coming
in less than a minute...
and, soon... it's a second...
and, now, I am in it!

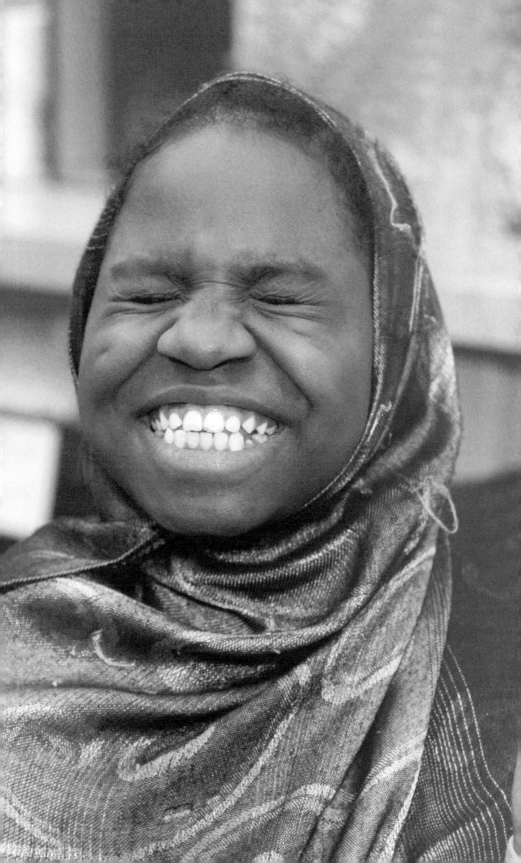

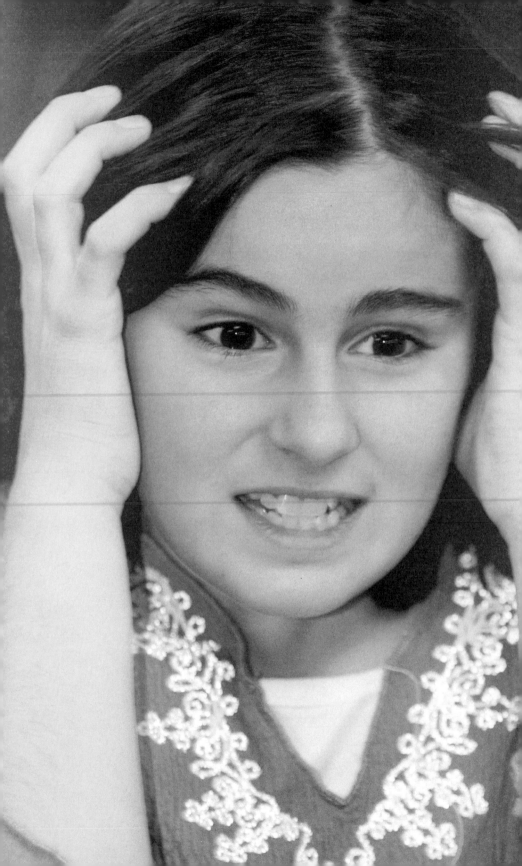

Aaaaa!

Aaaaa!
I don't believe it!
I've overslept! It's late!

Aaaaa!
No time for breakfast!
It's already twenty past eight!

Aaaaa!
I can't finish my homework!
Or study for my test!

Aaaaa!
I'll have to run to school!
I don't have time to get dressed!

Aaaaa!
My family has overslept too!
"WAKE UP, EVERYONE, RIGHT AWAY!"

Aaaaa!
Now I remember...

today is Saturday.

Summer Brains

Summer is a happy dream—
a speedy change of clothes.
A time to sleep, and race, and keep
some sand between your toes.

When school is finally over and
you've tackled every test,
you need to pull the power plug
and give your brain a rest.

Your cranium needs time to crash,
and sigh, and snooze, and snore—
forgetting all the stuff it learned,
to make some room for more.

Abdi

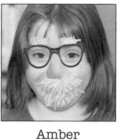

Amber

Anna

Brian

Clare

Thanks to the Crew!

Elina

Elisa

Emma

Erica

Georgia

Haedyn

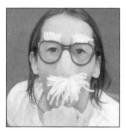

Hailee

Hien

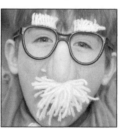

Holden

Iris

Jake

Kayla

Lauren

Morgan

Nathan

Ryan

Safia

Sophia

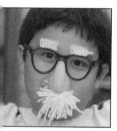

Steven

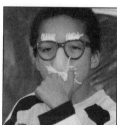

Taylor

In a poem,
like on faces,
magic happens
in quite small
places.

Tobias

Vina

Win

Pete

Ted

Ted Scheu

Ted Scheu (rhymes with "poetry guy") is a popular children's poet, teacher, and very-funny-kid-in-a-grown-up's-body. His poems are published widely in anthologies and in his own collections, including "I Froze My Mother", and "I Threw My Brother Out". Ted's joys in life (besides writing and reading poems) are being with his family, playing in the outdoors, and traveling the world, which he does a lot as a visiting author/teacher—inspiring young writers (like you!) to find their own voices in poetry. In fact, he'd love to come to your school anytime. Learn a lot more at his web site: **www.poetryguy.com**. Ted lives in Middlebury, Vermont.

Peter Lourie

Peter Lourie is a true renaissance man—explorer/adventurer, anthropologist, photographer, and teacher, as well as a well-known children's author. In his many award-winning books, he takes you to some of the most remote and rugged regions of the world including the Amazon, the Arctic, and everywhere wild in between. His "River Series," for readers age 9 and up, is published by Boyds Mills Press. Learn more about him at his web site **www.peterlourie.com**. Peter lives with his family in Weybridge, Vermont.

Winslow Colwell

Winslow Colwell is a most-marvelously-multi-talented designer of books, kites, and all things designable—many of which can be found at his web site at **www.wcolwell.com**. When he's not using his magic to design things he loves to read and tell stories to his daughter, and to listen to hers. Win and his family live in Ripton, Vermont.

Dear Reader,

Do you have some great poems that you have written? Why not add your poems to my collection right here!

Or, if you'd like me to read one of your poems, send your one favorite poem (just one!) to me (at my web site at www.poetryguy.com/kids.php), and I might just publish it there so the whole world can enjoy it!

I'd love to get a poem from you.

Cheers and Chuckles,

Ted

Need more copies of "I Tickled My Teachers" for your favorite 5,000 friends and relatives?

1. For super-speedy delivery, go to Ted's web site at **www.poetryguy.com** and push the "Order Books!" link, and you will be zoomed right to the publisher.

2. Fly over to Ted's web site at **www.poetryguy.com**, print out an order form, then snail-mail it to Ted. If you order directly from Ted, he can sign the books for you. Please let him know exactly how you'd like him to inscribe them, when you order.

You may also just send a check by mail for $12.95 (US$) for each book to Ted Scheu, PO Box 564, Middlebury, VT 05753, USA. Please include $3.00 (US) for postage and handling for up to four books, and $3.00 for each four books after that. To order from outside the US, go to #1 above.

3. Or you can surf right over to **amazon.com**, or **barnesandnoble.com**, or **borders.com** and order the book there.

4. Politely ask your wonderful local bookstore order the book for you.

Thanks!